HALLOWEEN JOKES FOR KIDS

Ghostly Giggles For Little Monsters To Enjoy And Have Fun | Kids Joke Book Ages 7-12

Adventure Kids Press

Copyright © 2023 by Adventure Kids Press. All Right Reserved.
ISBN: 979-8862027563

Under no circumstances, no part of this publication may be reproduced, distributed, or transmitted in any form or by any means, including photocopying, recording, or other electronic or mechanical methods, or by any information storage and retrieval system without the prior written permission of the copyright holder.

The information in this book is accurate and complete, however, the author and the publisher do not warrant the accuracy of the information, text and graphics contained within the book due to the rapidly changing nature of science, research, known and unknown facts and internet. The author and the publisher do not hold any responsibility for errors, omissions or contrary interpretation of the subject matter herein. This book is presented solely for motivational and informational purposes only.

CONTENTS

I. HALLOWEEN JOKES 6

II. GHOST JOKES 28

III. PUMPKIN JOKES 37

IV. SKELETON JOKES 47

V. WITCH JOKES 57

VI. VAMPIRE JOKES 67

VII. ZOMBIE JOKES 74

VIII. KNOCK-KNOCK JOKES 80

"A day without LAUGHTER is a day WASTED."

Charles Chaplin

INTRODUCTION

Halloween is a time of spooktacular fun, family gatherings, and time-honored traditions. The air buzzes with the scent of autumn leaves and freshly carved pumpkins, accompanied by the delightful shrieks and giggles of kids in costumes, trick-or-treating. What could add more spirit to this eerie season than a hearty chuckle?

Introducing our side-splitting Halloween joke book for kids! Overflowing with "boo-larious" jokes, this collection is designed to bewitch young minds and leave them howling with laughter. Whether they're beginner readers or already adept at delivering a punchline, our Halloween-themed quips will keep them spellbound for hours.

In a world that often seems overwhelmingly serious, we believe that laughter and fun are crucial for children's well-being. That's why we've concocted this Halloween joke book to add a splash of humor to your family's All Hallows' Eve festivities. So gather your little ghouls and goblins around and get ready to chuckle because when it comes to tickling funny bones, not even the Great Pumpkin can beat us!

Our Halloween jokes aren't just amusing; they also help kids refine their sense of humor and bolster their language skills. Crafting and delivering jokes are valuable social abilities that empower kids to build confidence and socialize more easily. Plus, our themed jokes offer an entertaining way for kids to learn about Halloween folklore and traditions.

The soul of our Halloween joke book is the timeless joy of spending quality moments with those who mean the most to us. These treasured connections lay the foundation for lifelong relationships, and what better way to fortify them than with laughter? So, if you're planning a Halloween party, joining a costume parade, or just looking for some seasonal fun at home, our jokes offer the perfect touch of whimsy to create everlasting memories.

With our Halloween joke book, your gatherings will be packed with laughs and memorable moments. Whether you're hosting a costume party, embarking on a trick-or-treat adventure, or merely enjoying a quiet evening at home, our jokes offer a frightfully fun way to liven up the celebration. So stir the cauldron and let's get ready for a howling good time!

1.
HALLOWEEN JOKES

WHAT KIND OF STONES
DO GHOSTS COLLECT?

Tombstones.

WHEN DO COWS TRANSFORM
INTO WEREWOLVES?

During the full moooooon.

DID YOU HEAR ABOUT THE ZOMBIE
THAT TOOK A REST?

It was dead tired.

WHAT DID THE GHOST
SAY WHEN IT FELL DOWN?

I got a boo-boo.

WHY DO ALL WITCHES
WEAR NAME TAGS?

To tell which witch is which.

WHAT WOULD THE HEADLESS
HORSEMAN DO IN SCHOOL?

He would want to get
a-head in life.

WHO DID THE TERRIFYING GHOST INVITE TO HIS PARTY?

Any old friend he could dig up!

HOW DO VAMPIRES TRAVEL ON HALLOWEEN?

On blood vessels.

WHAT DID THE FISHERMAN SAY ON HALLOWEEN?

Trick or trout.

DID YOU HEAR ABOUT
THE CRAZY VAMPIRE?

He was totally batty.

WHERE DO GHOSTS BUY STAMPS?

At the ghost office.

WHAT DO HE SPOOKY GHOSTS WEAR
WHEN THEIR EYESIGHT GETS BLURRED?

Spooktacles.

WHAT IS THE FAVORITE CEREAL OF A ZOMBIE?

Rice Creepies.

WHAT WOULD BE A REAL PAIN IN THE NECK?

Being kissed by a vampire.

HOW CAN YOU TELL WHEN A VAMPIRE HAS VISITED THE BAKERY?

All the jelly has been sucked out of the jelly muffins.

HOW DO YOU KNOW
VAMPIRES LOVE BASEBALL?

They turn into bats every night.

WHY WOULD THE SKELETON
CLIMB UP THE TREE?

Because a dog was after his bones!

WHERE DO GHOSTS GO
ON VACATION?

To The Dead Sea!

WHERE DO GHOSTS
GO ON HOLIDAYS?

The Boohamas.

WHAT DOES A DRAGON
EAT FOR A SNACK?

Firecrackers.

WHY ARE GHOSTS ALWAYS
SO BAD AT TELLING LIES?

Because one can see
right through them.

WHY DIDN'T THE SKELETON GO TO PROM?

He had no body to go with.

WHAT DID ONE GHOST SAY TO THE OTHER?

Get a life!

WHERE DO BABY GHOSTS GO DURING THE DAY?

Day-scare.

WHAT DAY DO GHOSTS DO THEIR HOWLING?

On Moan-day!

WHAT DOES A PANDA GHOST EAT?

Bam-BOO!

WHAT STORY DOES LITTLE WITCH LIKE TO HEAR AT BEDTIME?

Ghoul-di-locks and the Three Scares.

WHAT DID ONE PUMPKIN SAY
TO THE OTHER?

Orange, you glad I'm here.

WHY DID THE PUMPKIN MOVE
BACK HOME?

To get in touch with its roots.

WHAT'S A VAMPIRE'S
FAVORITE DANCE?

The "vamp"ire waltz!

WHAT DO YOU CALL
A DANCING GHOST?

Polka-haunt-us.

WHERE IS THE BEST PLACE
TO PARTY ON HALLOWEEN?

The g-RAVE-yard.

WHY WOULD THE BABY WRAP ITSELF
IN WHITE CLOTH STRIPS?

It is trying to be
just like its mummy.

WHAT IS A VAMPIRE'S FAVORITE FRUIT?

A neck-tarine.

WHAT DO YOU GET WHEN YOU CROSS FALINE WITH A GHOST?

Falloo.

DO MUMMIES ENJOY BEING MUMMIES?

Of corpse!

WHY DO GHOSTS MAKE
THE BEST CHEERLEADERS?

Because they have spirit.

WHY DO GHOSTS LIKE TO
HANG OUT AT BARS?

Because of all of the Boos.

WHY DO GHOSTS DESPISE
THE RAIN ON HALLOWEEN?

It dampens their spirits.

WHO WON THE SKELETON BEAUTY CONTEST?

No body.

WHAT PANTS DO GHOSTS WEAR TO TRICK OR TREAT?

Boo jeans.

WHAT HALLOWEEN CANDY IS NEVER ON TIME FOR THE PARTY?

Choco-LATE!

WHAT DO YOU CALL
TWO WITCHES LIVING TOGETHER?

Broommates.

WHAT POSITION DOES
A GHOST PLAY IN HOCKEY?

Ghoulie.

WHAT MAKES TRICK OR TREAT
WITH TWIN WITCHES
SO CHALLENGING?

You never know which
witch is which!

WHAT DO OWLS SAY WHEN
THEY GO TRICK OR TREATING?

"Happy Owl-ween!"

WHO DID FRANKENSTEIN
GO TRICK-OR-TREATING WITH?

His ghoul friend.

WHAT DOES BIGFOOT SAY
WHEN HE ASKS FOR CANDY?

"Trick-or-feet!"

WHAT DO GHOSTS GIVE
TO TRICK-OR-TREATERS?

Booberries!

WHAT DO BIRDS SAY
ON HALLOWEEN?

"Trick or tweet!"

WHAT SHOULD YOU DO
IF THERE'S A ZOMBIE ATTACK?

Play dead.

WHERE DO GHOSTS BUY THEIR HALLOWEEN CANDY?

At the ghost-ery store!

WHAT DO YOU CALL A VAMPIRE THAT'S ALWAYS ON THE PHONE?

A bloodsucker!

WHY DON'T SKELETONS EVER GO AS TRICK-OR-TREATERS?

Because they have no-body to go with.

WHY DIDN'T CINDERELLA
MAKE THE SOCCER TEAM?

Her coach was a pumpkin.

WHERE SHOULD YOU HIDE IF
YOU'RE BEING CHASED BY ZOMBIES?

The living room.

HOW DO MUMMIES HIDE?

They use masking tape.

HOW DO PUMPKINS
QUIT SMOKING?

They use a pumpkin patch.

WHY A ZOMBIE LOSES
AN ARGUMENT?

It doesn't have a leg to stand on.

WHAT SPRAY DO GHOSTS USE
TO STYLE THEIR HAIR?

Scare-spray.

WHAT ALARM SOUND DO YOU HEAR
WHEN DRAGONS EAT SPICY FOOD?

A fire alarm.

DID YOU HEAR ABOUT
THE ZOMBIE WHO LOST THE RACE?

It came in dead last.

WHAT SHOULDN'T YOU SERVE
A VAMPIRE FOR DINNER?

Steak.

II. GHOST JOKES

WHAT KIND OF MUFFINS
DO GHOSTS PREFER?

Boo-berry.

WHAT KIND OF SHOES
DO GHOSTS WEAR?

Boo-ts.

DID YOU HEAR ABOUT
LAST NIGHT'S GHOST PARTY?

It was loud enough to wake the dead.

WHY DID THE GHOST RIDE THE ELEVATOR?

To lift its spirit.

WHAT'S A GHOST'S FAVORITE DINNER?

Spook-etti.

WHY DON'T GHOSTS DO STANDUP COMEDY?

They always get booed.

WHY DON'T GHOSTS SHOWER?

It dampens their spirits.

HOW DO GHOSTS APPLY FOR JOBS?

They fill out apparitions.

WHERE DO GHOSTS SHOP?

Boo-tiques.

WHICH POSITION DO GHOSTS PLAY IN FOOTBALL?

Ghoul-keeper.

HOW DO GHOSTS UNLOCK DOORS?

With spoo-keys.

WHAT'S A TEENAGE GHOST'S FAVORITE SONG?

Ghouls Just Wanna Have Fun.

HOW DO GHOSTS PREDICT
THE FUTURE?

They check their horror-scope.

WHAT DO GHOSTS TURN ON
IN SUMMER?

The scare-conditioner!

WHY DID THE GHOST
CROSS THE ROAD?

He wanted to return from
the other side.

HOW DO GHOSTS GO FROM ONE FLOOR TO ANOTHER?

By scare-case!

HOW DO GHOSTS WASH THEIR HAIR?

With sham-boo!

ON WHICH DAY ARE GHOSTS MOST SCARY?

Fright-day!

WHY DO GHOSTS PICK THEIR NOSES?

To get the boo-gers!

WHAT DID ONE GHOST SAY TO THE OTHER GHOST?

Do you believe in people?

WHAT DO GHOSTS EAT FOR DESSERT?

Ice scream.

HOW DO YOU KNOW
IF A GHOST IS SAD?

He is boo-hooing.

WHAT IS A SPOOK'S
FAVORITE RIDE?

A roller-ghoster!

WHAT'S A GHOST'S
FAVORITE PLAY?

Romeo and Ghoul-iet.

III.

PUMPKIN JOKES

WHO RULES THE PUMPKIN PATCH?

The pump-king.

WHAT KIND OF PUMPKINS WORK AT A POOL?

Life-gourds.

HOW DO LITTLE PUMPKINS CROSS THE ROAD?

With the help of a crossing gourd.

WHY DID THE PUMPKIN
GO TO JAIL?

It had a bad seed.

WHAT'S A PUMPKIN'S
FAVORITE FRUIT?

Orange.

HOW DO YOU FIX A
JACK-O-LANTERN THAT'S BROKEN?

No worries - let's give
it pumpkin patch!

WHAT KIND OF CANINE DO PUMPKINS PREFER?

Gourd-dogs.

WHAT'S A PUMPKIN'S FAVORITE SPORT?

Squash.

WHY DO PUMPKINS BAR HOP?

To get smashed.

HOW DO PUMPKINS QUIT SMOKING?

They use a pumpkin patch.

WHAT DO YOU CALL A FEMALE PUMPKIN?

A pump-queen.

HOW DO PUMPKINS GET PAID?

With pumpkin bread.

WHY DIDN'T CINDERELLA MAKE THE SOCCER TEAM?

Her coach was a pumpkin.

WHAT DO LITTLE BOYS AND GHOULS STUDY IN ALGEBRA?

Pumpkin pi.

WHY DID THE GHOST CROSS THE ROAD?

He wanted to return from the other side.

WHAT DO YOU GET WHEN YOU DROP A PUMPKIN?

Squash.

WHAT DID THE HAPPY PUMPKIN SAY?

"Life is gourd."

WHAT'S A PUMPKIN'S FAVORITE WESTERN?

The Gourd, the Bad, and the Ugly.

WHAT DOES A CARVED
PUMPKIN CELEBRATE?

Hollow-een.

HOW DO GOURDS GROW
BIG AND STRONG?

Pumpkin iron.

WHY DID THE PUMPKIN TAKE
A DETOUR?

To avoid a seedy part of town.

WHAT'S A PUMPKIN'S FAVORITE GENRE?

Pulp fiction.

WHY WAS THE GOURD SO GOSSIPY?

To give 'em pumpkin to talk about.

WHAT DID THE PUMPKIN SAY TO ITS CARVER?

Cut it out!

WHERE DOES A PUMPKIN PREACH?

From the pulp-it.

WHAT'S THE BEST THING TO PUT INTO A PUMPKIN PIE?

Your teeth.

WHAT DO YOU CALL A YOUNG PUMPKIN?

A pump-kid.

IV. SKELETON JOKES

WHAT'S A SKELETON'S FAVORITE MUSICAL INSTRUMENT?

The trom-bone.

WHY DID THE SKELETON SKIP THE PROM?

It had no body to go with.

WHAT DID THE SKELETON BRING TO THE BARBECUE?

Spare ribs.

WHY THE SKELETONS DON'T LIKE THE COLD WEATHER?

It's bone-chilling.

HOW DO SKELETONS START THEIR CARS?

With skeleton keys.

WHY DON'T SKELETONS SKYDIVE?

They don't have the stomach for it.

WHAT'S A SKELETON'S FAVORITE SONG?

"Bad to the Bone."

WHAT DO YOU CALL A SKELETON THAT WON'T DO ANY WORK?

Lazy bones.

WHY'D THE SKELETON GO TO THE GROCERY STORE?

Its pantry was down to the bare bones.

WHY DO SKELETONS HAVE LOW SELF-ESTEEM?

They have no body to love.

WHAT DO SKELETONS FLY AROUND IN?

A scareplane or a skelecopter.

WHY DID THE SKELETON LAUGH?

Something tickled its funny bone.

WHY DID THE SKELETON CLIMB THE TREE?

A dog was chasing him.

WHY DON'T SKELETONS GO TRICK-OR-TREATING?

They don't have the guts.

WHAT DO SKELETON DOGS EAT?

Milk bones.

HOW DO SKELETONS SENSE WHAT IS GOING TO HAPPEN?

They can feel it in their bones.

WHO IS THE WORLD'S BEST SKELETON DETECTIVE?

Sherlock Bones.

WHY DO SKELETONS ARGUE?

They always have a bone to pick.

WHO WON THE SKELETON BEAUTY CONTEST?

No body.

WHAT DO YOU CALL A CLEANING SKELETON?

A grim sweeper.

WHAT IS A SKELETON'S FAVOURITE DRINK?

A full-bodied wine.

WHAT DO YOU CALL
A DUMB SKELETON?

Bonehead.

WHAT'S THE PREFERRED INSTRUMENT
FOR SKELETONS IN THE BAND?

The saxo-bone.

WHAT DO YOU CALL A TIRED
SKELETON ON HALLOWEEN?

The Drowsy Reaper.

WHAT DO SKELETONS SAY
WHEN HAVING DINNER?

"Bone-Appetit."

WHO IS SKELETONS' FAVORITE
HISTORICAL FIGURE?

Napoleon Bone-aparte.

WHY DON'T SKELETONS LIKE
HALLOWEEN CANDY?

They don't have the
stomach for it.

V. WITCH JOKES

WHAT DO WITCHES' STUDY IN SCHOOL?

Spelling.

WHY DID THE WITCH CANCEL HER SPEECH?

There was a frog in her throat.

WHERE DO WITCHES PARK?

In the broom closet.

DID YOU HEAR ABOUT THE WITCH
THAT CAN'T WIN AT ANY SPORT?

It was a dry spell.

HAVE YOU HEARD ABOUT THE WITCH
WHO GOT SCHOOL DETENTION?

She was ex-spelled.

WHY DOES AN ANGRY WITCH
LEAVE HER BROOM AT HOME?

She doesn't want
to fly off the handle.

WHAT IS THE PERFECT BIRTHDAY GIFT FOR A WITCH?

A spellbinding bangle!

WHAT DO YOU CALL TWO WITCHES WHO LIVE TOGETHER?

Broommates.

HOW DO WITCHES ON BROOMSTICKS DRINK THEIR HOT TEA?

Very carefully!

WHERE DOES THE WITCH'S FROG SIT?

On a toadstool.

WHAT DO WITCHES EAT FOR LUNCH?

Sand-witches.

WHAT'S A WITCHES' PICK-UP LINE?

Hey, you've got hex appeal!

WHAT DID THE WITCH DO WHEN HER BROOMSTICK BROKE?

She witch-hiked home.

WHAT DO WITCHES PUT ON TO GO TRICK-OR-TREATING?

Mas-scare-a.

FOR HOW LONG DWITCHES RIDE THEIR BROOMSTICKS ON A COLD NIGHT?

For just a short spell.

WHAT DO YOU CALL A WITCH THAT LIVES AT THE BEACH?

A sand witch!

HOW DOES A WITCH PLAY LOUD MUSIC?

On her broom box.

WHAT DO WITCHES RACE ON?

Vroomsticks!

FOR WHAT SERVICE DO WITCHES
ASK WHEN AT A HOTEL?

Broom service.

HOW DO YOU MAKE
A WITCH SCRATCH?

Take away the W.

WHY DID THE WITCH TAKE A NAP?

She needed to rest a spell.

HOW DOES A WITCH TELL THE TIME?

She looks at her witch-watch!

HOW IS A WITCH LIKE A CANDLE?

They're both wicked.

WHY DID THE WITCH TRAVEL ON A BROOM?

She couldn't afford a vacuum cleaner!

WHAT IS EVIL, UGLY
AND BOUNCES?

A witch on a pogo broom.

WHAT DO YOU GET WHEN YOU CROSS
A WITCH'S CAT WITH A CANARY?

A cat with a full belly.

WHAT HAPPENS TO WITCHES
WHEN IT RAINS?

They get wet just like
everyone else!

VI. VAMPIRE JOKES

DID YOU HEAR ABOUT
THE VAMPIRE FEUD?

There was bad blood.

WHY DID THE VAMPIRE GET
GLASSES?

It was as blind as a bat.

HOW CAN YOU SPOT A
WEALTHY VAMPIRE?

It has blue blood.

WHY DOES THE VAMPIRE GO TO THE DENTIST?

It has a bat breath.

WHAT DO YOU CALL VAMPIRE SIBLINGS?

Blood brothers.

WHERE DO VAMPIRES DEPOSIT THEIR PAYCHECKS?

At the blood bank.

WHAT HAPPENS WHEN
VAMPIRES GET MAD?

It makes their blood boil.

WHAT'S A VAMPIRE'S FAVORITE
KIND OF DOG?

A bloodhound.

WHY WAS THE MATH BOOK ALWAYS
AFRAID OF THE VAMPIRE?

Because it had
too many problems!

WHY DID THE VAMPIRE GO
TO THE DOCTOR?

It was a coffin.

WHY DO VAMPIRES AVOID
THE COLD?

They don't want to get frostbite.

HOW DO VAMPIRE FOOTBALLERS
GET THE MUD OFF?

They all get in the bat tub.

DID YOU HEAR ABOUT
THE VAMPIRE ROMANCE?

It was love at first bite.

WHY DON'T VAMPIRES GET
INVITED TO PARTIES?

They're a pain in the neck.

WHAT DO YOU CALL A VAMPIRE
WITH NO TEETH?

A gummy vampire!

WHAT DO YOU CALL A VAMPIRE
WHO TELLS JOKES?

A punpire!

WHAT DO YOU CALL A VAMPIRE THAT
LIVES IN A KITCHEN?

Chef Dracu-cook!

HOW DO VAMPIRES BRUSH
THEIR TEETH?

With fang paste!

VI. ZOMBIE JOKES

WHAT'S A ZOMBIE'S
PICK-UP LINE?

You're drop-dead gorgeous.

WHAT KIND OF MUSIC
DO ZOMBIES LISTEN TO?

The Grateful Dead.

WHERE DO ZOMBIES LIVE?

On a dead end.

WHAT DO YOU CALL IDENTICAL ZOMBIE TWINS?

Dead ringers.

DID YOU HEAR ABOUT THE ZOMBIE WHO LOST THE RACE?

It came in dead last.

DID YOU HEAR ABOUT THE ZOMBIE RECITAL?

The performance knocked 'em dead.

WHAT DO ZOMBIES ORDER
AT THE DELI?

Knuckle sandwich.

WHY DON'T ZOMBIES
EAT CLOWNS?

They taste funny.

WHERE SHOULD YOU HIDE IF YOU'RE
BEING CHASED BY ZOMBIES?

The living room.

WHY DID EVERYONE LEAVE
THE ZOMBIE PARTY?

It wasn't very lively.

WHAT KIND OF CARS
DO ZOMBIES DRIVE?

Monster trucks.

WHY DID THE ZOMBIE GET FIRED?

It missed
its dead-line.

WHAT DOES IT COST FOR A ZOMBIE TO BUY A NEW CAR?

It cost an arm and a leg.

DID YOU HEAR ABOUT THE ANGRY ZOMBIE?

It got bent out of shape.

WHY DID THE ZOMBIE TAKE A NAP?

It was dead on its feet.

VIII. KNOCK-KNOCK JOKES

KNOCK, KNOCK!
WHO'S THERE?

Howl. Howl who?
Howl-ween is here!

KNOCK, KNOCK!
WHO'S THERE?

Witch. Witch who?
Witch one of you has the candy?

KNOCK, KNOCK!
WHO'S THERE?

Owl. Owl who?
Correct.

KNOCK, KNOCK!
WHO'S THERE?

Twig. Twig who?
Twig or tweat.

KNOCK, KNOCK!
WHO'S THERE?

Ash. Ash who?
A zombie with a cold.

KNOCK, KNOCK!
WHO'S THERE?

Minnie. Minnie who?
Minnie people love Halloween.

KNOCK, KNOCK!
WHO'S THERE?

Ice cream. Ice cream who?
Ice cream at zombies.

KNOCK, KNOCK!
WHO'S THERE?

Bat. Bat who?
Bat you don't know
who's knocking!

KNOCK, KNOCK!
WHO'S THERE?

Avery. Avery who?
Avery scary ghost! Run!

KNOCK, KNOCK!
WHO'S THERE?

Creep. Creep who?
Creep it down, you'll
wake the dead.

KNOCK, KNOCK!
WHO'S THERE?

Witch. Witch who?
Gesundheit.

KNOCK, KNOCK!
WHO'S THERE?

Gwen. Gwen who?
Gwen, do you think Halloween
will be here?

KNOCK, KNOCK!
WHO'S THERE?

**Boo. Boo who?
Boo hoo, don't make a ghost cry.**

KNOCK, KNOCK!
WHO'S THERE?

**Phillip! Phillip who?
Phillip, my bag with
Halloween candy, please!**

KNOCK, KNOCK!
WHO'S THERE?

Ivana. Ivana who?
Ivana suck your blood, blah!

KNOCK, KNOCK!
WHO'S THERE?

Bean. Bean who?
Bean waiting for Halloween
all year long.

KNOCK, KNOCK!
WHO'S THERE?

**Boo. Boo who?
Don't cry! I didn't mean
to scare you.**

KNOCK, KNOCK!
WHO'S THERE?

**Witch! Witch who?
Witch one of you will give me
the most Halloween candy?**

KNOCK, KNOCK!
WHO'S THERE?

Eddy. Eddy who?
Eddy-body will do for a zombie.

KNOCK, KNOCK!
WHO'S THERE?

Al. Al who?
Al goes home
after
trick-or-treating.

KNOCK, KNOCK!
WHO'S THERE?

**Ash. Ash who?
A zombie with a cold.**

KNOCK, KNOCK!
WHO'S THERE?

**Howl! Howl who?
Howl, you will know unless
you open the door!**

KNOCK, KNOCK!
WHO'S THERE?

Ben! Ben who?
Ben is waiting to
get candy all day!

Made in the USA
Las Vegas, NV
07 October 2023

78722340R00052